Mindfulness

by Mari Schuh

Pebble Explore is published by Pebble, an imprint of Capstone
1710 Roe Crest Drive
North Mankato, Minnesota 56003
www.capstonepub.com

Library of Congress Cataloging-in-Publication Data
Names: Schuh, Mari C., 1975- author.
Title: Mindfulness / by Mari Schuh.
Description: North Mankato, Minnesota : Pebble/Capstone Press,
[2021] | Series: Health and my body | Includes bibliographical
references and index. | Audience: Ages 6-8 | Audience: Grades 2-3 |
Summary: "Life is busy and full of stress. It's important to slow down.
Take your time and notice what's going on around you. Being present
in the moment can help you be more focused, patient, and self-
aware. So take a deep breath, smile, and read on to learn more about
mindfulness"—Provided by publisher.
Identifiers: LCCN 2020032582 (print) | LCCN 2020032583 (ebook)
| ISBN 9781977132208 (hardcover) | ISBN 9781977133236
(paperback) | ISBN 9781977159359 (pdf) | ISBN 9781977159366
(kindle edition)
Subjects: LCSH: Mindfulness (Psychology)—Juvenile literature. |
Meditation for children—Juvenile literature.
Classification: LCC BF637.M56 S345 2021 (print) | LCC BF637.M56
(ebook) | DDC 155.4/1913—dc23
LC record available at https://lccn.loc.gov/2020032582
LC ebook record available at https://lccn.loc.gov/2020032583

Image Credits
iStockphoto: ActionPics, 18, Hiraman, 10, lithiumcloud, 11;
Shutterstock: ANURAK PONGPATIMET, 25, Dragon Images, 12,
fizkes, 26, Lucky Business, 15, michaeljung, 27, Monkey Business
Images, 17, 20, 23, Neirfy, 7, pedalist, 5, photonova, design element
throughout, Regreto, 21, RodfaiStudio, 19, wavebreakmedia, 9, 22,
XiXinXing, Cover, Yiorgos GR, 13, Zurijeta, 29

Editorial Credits
Editor: Christianne Jones; Designer: Sarah Bennett; Media Researcher:
Morgan Walters; Production Specialist: Laura Manthe

Printed and bound in the United States of America. PO3837

Table of Contents

Bold words are in the glossary.

What Is Mindfulness?

Think about how you feel right now. Do you feel calm or worried? Are you tired or full of energy? Are you breathing quickly or slowly?

Mindfulness is a skill. Being **mindful** is about being aware. It's about noticing your thoughts and feelings right now. When you are mindful, you are aware of what your senses are telling you. You pay **attention** to what is happening in the moment.

When you are mindful, you are **focused**. You don't try to do lots of things at the same time. When you choose to do one thing, you do not feel **stressed**. Instead, you feel calm as you focus on what you're doing. You take your time and slow down.

Pay attention to your body. Lie down. Close your eyes. Tighten every muscle in your body. Squeeze your hands. Squeeze your toes! How do you feel? After a few seconds, relax. How do you feel now?

Breathing

You can calm down and focus. **Meditation** can help. Try it! Find a quiet spot. Sit down and close your eyes. Be still and quiet. Slowly take in air through your nose. Then slowly let out the air through your mouth. Can you feel your chest and belly move?

Your mind might wander. You might start thinking of something else, like school or friends. That's OK. Just tell yourself to think only about your breathing.

Now try some belly breathing. Find a pillow or a stuffed animal. Lie down on your back. Put the pillow or toy on your belly.

Take deep breaths using your belly. Take in air through your nose. Fill up your belly like a balloon. Then let out the air through your mouth.

Look at the pillow or toy on your belly. See it go up. See it go down. How do you feel?

Eating

To be mindful when you eat, try to slow down. It's easy to eat too quickly. Focus on your food. Turn off the TV. Put away phones and computers. You will enjoy your food more.

Be sure you are hungry before you eat. Sometimes people eat when they are bored. They might eat when they are sad. Listen to your body. Is your stomach growling? Do you feel weak? If so, it's probably time to eat.

Use your senses when you eat. Sit down and look at your food. What colors and shapes do you see? How does your food smell? Take a bite. What flavors do you taste?

Take your time. Chew slowly. Put down your fork after each bite. Take a drink. Do you really need more food? Wait about 20 minutes to decide. It can take your body that much time to tell you if you are full.

Playing

Learn to be mindful when you are having fun too. A nature walk is the perfect way to practice being mindful.

Use your senses. Listen closely. Do you hear birds chirping? Do you hear dogs barking? Find rocks and leaves. Touch them. How do they feel? Look up at the sky. What do the clouds look like? Do you see any birds? Take a deep breath. What do you smell?

You can be mindful when you play sports too. Aliya plays baseball. It is her turn to bat. She is focused. She closely watches the ball. Aliya is calm and ready. She pays attention so she can hit the ball.

Sometimes you're mindful without thinking about it. Joe plays basketball outside. The traffic is loud. But he doesn't hear the noise. He is focused on the game. He shoots the ball. Joe scores!

How Mindfulness Can Help You

Being mindful can help you at school. Mindfulness can make it easier to remember things. It can help you plan and **organize**. You learn to focus. You will be less distracted.

Mindfulness can help you control your **emotions**. You learn to think in a positive way. You get upset less often. You can stay calm when you are under stress. Then you might make better choices.

Being mindful can help you get along better with people. It can help you be patient and kind. You can be a better listener. When people are mindful, they are more aware of other people's feelings. This helps them think of others.

Dawn started a new school. She is nervous. Santos sees how Dawn is feeling. He listens to her. He is mindful of her feelings. Santos understands how Dawn is feeling and includes her in his study group.

Practice!

Being mindful is not easy. We are often busy and rushed. It takes practice to be mindful. You can make it a **habit**. Take time to be mindful every day. Stop what you are doing. Think about how your mind and body are feeling. You can do this any time!

Sammy is getting ready for school. She gets up early so she doesn't feel rushed. She takes her time eating. She takes a few deep breaths. Sammy notices that she feels calm. She is ready to go to school.

Mindfulness isn't only for tough times. Practice being aware during good times too. Did you say something nice to a friend? Stop to think about how that made you feel. Did you win a game? How does your body feel? Write down your feelings.

Jamal and Shay won first place at the science fair. They are excited! They stop to listen to their bodies. Their hearts are beating quickly. They have lots of energy. Jamal and Shay feel happy but in control.

Practice being mindful every day. You can practice at home and school. Use all of your senses. Take time to notice how your body feels. Be aware of what you are thinking right now. Soon, you will get better at paying attention.

Learn to slow down. Do one thing at a time. Stop and breathe. Then you will be calm and focused!

Glossary

attention (uh-TEN-shuhn)—the ability to focus and concentrate

emotion (i-MOH-shuhn)—a strong feeling; people have and show emotions such as happiness, sadness, fear, and anger

focus (FOH-kuss)—to keep all your attention on one thing

habit (HAB-it)—something that you do often

meditation (MED-i-tay-shun)—thinking deeply and quietly; to relax the mind and body by a regular program of mental exercise

mindful (MIND-full)—being aware of your body, mind, and feelings in the present moment

organize (OR-guh-nize)—to arrange things neatly and in order

stress (STRESS)—strain or pressure

Read More

Bullis, Amber. *Mindfulness at School.* Minneapolis: Jump!, Inc., 2020.

Kalman, Bobbie. *Be Mindful!: Be Here Now.* New York: Crabtree Publishing Company, 2019.

Verde, Susan. *I Am Peace: A Book of Mindfulness.* New York: Abrams Books, 2017.

Internet Sites

BrainPOP: Mindfulness
jr.brainpop.com/health/feelings/mindfulness

KidsHealth: Mindfulness
kidshealth.org/en/kids/mindfulness.html

Positive Psychology
positivepsychology.com/mindfulness-for-kids

Index